SNAP OUT OF IT!

A Collection of Madge Madigan's Columns
from Rochester Woman Magazine

MADGE MADIGAN

Cheryl,
Thanks for
all you do!

Best,
Madge
Madigan

DEDICATION

To my children: Jack, Libby and Abby. To the wonderful folks at Rochester Woman Magazine. Of course the great people of the city of Rochester, NY. And all the people along the way who's actions prompted me to write these columns. God bless your hearts.

CONTENTS

ACKNOWLEDGMENTS

Barb McSpadden for creating the awesome cover of this book and her guidance. All the readers of Rochester Woman Magazine for giving me an audience. Amy White for helping me find my purpose. My Mom and Dad who gave me life and raised me with great values, most importantly – to love everyone without prejudice, and treat them as you would want to be treated.

1 HOW TO MAKE THE HOLIDAYS NOT SUCK

I'm Madge Madigan and welcome to my column. I will be planted here on a regular basis dispensing knowledge and useless facts and imparting words of wisdom that I obviously learned from someone else. You can find more stories that will make you smile and realize you're not alone in wading through the crap in life, in my book "When Life Gives You Lemons... At Least You Won't Get Scurvy!"

What better time than November to discuss the ensuing holiday marathon that we will all try to endure? If you don't manage to stress yourself out in some way, shape or form, someone else will. Oh I can pretty much guaran-damn-tee it. Between Veteran's Day, Thanksgiving, Hanukkah, Feast of the Immaculate Conception, Festivus, Christmas, Boxing Day, Kwanzaa, New Year's Eve, New Year's Day, Mawlid Un Nabi, the Epiphany, and any other thing I left out... something is going to set you off.

First and foremost, I would just like to make my stand on the holidays perfectly clear...
IT'S NOT A COMPETITION, PEOPLE! IT'S JUST A HOLIDAY! A DAY TO BE ENJOYED!

I see so many Facebook and Twitter posts every holiday season that state how stressed out people are with the holidays. I was about to call the suicide prevention hotline for one woman, she seemed so on edge. I also saw another post that was so smug about how far ahead she was of the game with all her shopping and wrapping, I wanted to throw a shoe at her.

There's so much talk on social media and in real life about who's going where and who's making what. The whole week before Thanksgiving is all food talk, all the time. I don't get myself worked up, ya' know why? Because I... don't make much. Best way to handle it. And I do everything on Thanksgiving Day. I'm not making homemade this and homemade that all week, I just do the turkey with my special basting slop, I do make homemade mashed potatoes (how hard is that?), I cut up a yam, and I make that green bean casserole because the kids love it. Hey, don't judge! It's about making the comfort food that my kids like that have become traditions. If I wanted the froo-froo asparagus and pine nuts and junk, I'd go eat out. (which I love, by the way). Between the wine and the hot flashes, I sweat enough that day, I'm not doing any more than I have to!... And that is why I buy my pies too.

Then Christmas, oh my god with the Christmas! You know, I've never heard any of my Jewish friends stress out about Hanukkah. Ok, I've only heard one Jewish friend complain but it was mostly about having to get on a plane to see her parents that happen to be at the further end of the AARP spectrum, who like to eat the early bird at Howard Johnson's then go to bed at 7:30 every night while she's there. But her bitching is usually just purely for comedic value anyway. However, she never complained about buying presents and decorating. Jewish folks make it simple, no tree, no decorations, one simple light fixture, eight days of presents so in case you forget something the first few nights... no pressure. Well, except there is a bit of food, but nary do I hear any complaining about all the schlepping to make it.

So back to the Christmas. Enough already! Enough with the buying and the wrapping, and the baking, and the decorating and the parties... no wait, the parties can stay. It's one thing if you really love this stuff, then do it, just don't be a martyr all over the place about it. Trust me, nobody likes a martyr.

You know how to survive these holidays? Just chillax. What gets done, will get done. No one will notice that you forgot to put out your Wayne Newton dressed as Santa statuette. No one will notice that you only made a batch of sugar cookies and not peanut butter cookies. The kids won't care if you wrapped their stocking stuffers or not. Just try to enjoy the spirit of Christmas, family and friends. (yes, even if you hate your family)

And speaking of that... what if you are thrust into a situation where you have to be with people you don't particularly care for, nay even hate? Suck it up and deal. Be nice and civil. Remember you're not the only person in the room. I know you have your pride but why ruin everyone else's holiday as well as yours? Don't be antagonistic, stay away from touchy subjects and hold your tongue if you are provoked. That will beat the hell out of having to post bail on Thanksgiving night for aggravated assault. I know some women have fantasies about exacting revenge on their mother-in-law that might look like Alexis and Krystle from "Dynasty", rolling around slapping and ripping out shoulder pads. But most of the time those things end up looking like Snookie and Angela pulling out weaves on "Jersey Shore" with their skirt over their head showing their butt in a thong. Not pretty. Next thing you know you're on an episode of "Cops."

As matter of fact, even if you like the people you will be spending the holiday with, just stay away from controversial topics all together that might start arguments – religion, politics, sex, and Grandma's will.

Back to the overdoing it and not being a competition with every other parent or homemaker in town... You might say, "What about the kids? It's important for the kids." Guess what? The kids will get over it; they don't need every gift under the sun or to live in a winter wonderland every day of the holidays. I believe you might be teaching your kids a far more valuable lesson in life if they don't get everything they want this year. I kid you not, there were years when things were rough being a single parent and my kids got construction paper or earrings or mittens from the Dollar Store. I cried and cried. Yes, I felt terrible that I couldn't give my children everything I wanted to, but my children have learned that life isn't fair and to be thankful for what they do get. I'd like to think I won't be raising a bunch of spoiled ingrates. However, as a loving Mother I wish I had the means to raise spoiled ingrates just so they could have nice things, but I realize the life lesson and not having ingrates is better and will last a lifetime, unlike an iPad or Beats by Dre.

Hey, didn't that Christmas angel say, "Peace on Earth, good will toward men"? THAT's what it's about! Please everyone, spread peace and good will to others, and accept peace yourself. That's really the key, peace within yourself; it feels wonderful and it's uncanny how it spreads to others.

Take a deep breath and relish the simple joys. And remember, you will not be put to death by lethal injection if the silverware isn't polished or the stuffing is dry or the kids wouldn't sit for the Christmas card photo. Merry Christmas, Happy Hanukkah, Happy Festivus, Happy Kwanza to all and to all a good night! And most importantly... Peace!

2 MY HOLIDAY IS BETTER THAN YOUR HOLIDAY

I ask myself sometimes, "Is nothing sacred anymore?" And I usually come up with the answer, "No, not really" and I don't mean that in a self-righteous Michelle Duggar kind of way, I mean it as wow, we just don't honor some stuff like we used to... but ya' know, it's a different world now.

I got to thinking this as the usual onslaught of holiday propaganda started cropping up. It first started with all the rumblings on social media about the pros and cons of Black Friday and the calls for public lynchings of CEOs of companies that would - *gasp* - be open on Thanksgiving Day. Which does seems a little crappy. Which by the way, did you ever notice no one really complains about stores not being closed on Christmas? It's because everyone is usually so sick of holidays and their family by then, they can't wait to get the hell out and go to the corner bar or movie theater. Well, and that there needs to be something open for the non-Christians as well. Hey, we are supposed to be a country that welcomes all, right? For decades my Jewish friends (not just characters in Woody Allen movies) just went out for Chinese and a movie on Christmas, it's just what you did.

Anyway, I was thinking back to when I was a kid in the 60's and 70's, nothing was ever open on Thanksgiving or Christmas. Heck, nothing was even open every Sunday back then! It seemed the whole country shut down to be with family and friends and honor and worship... whatever. I remember a strange eeriness to the empty streets on Thanksgiving or Christmas when we would go to pick up my Father's elderly cousin Agatha O'Connor, who didn't drive, to join us for the holiday meal. She had no other family left than my Father and she never married so she was kind of like my surrogate Grandmother. (Back then every Irish family had one old maid or bachelor relative that we all had to take care of, it was mandatory) Thinking back now though, it seemed like a magical time, the world, at least our corner of the world was quiet for a moment on that day.

And oh my God, if the phone rang and it wasn't my Grandmother or one of my older siblings who couldn't make it home for the holiday, you got the death stare to get off the phone. You were to say "Can't talk now", quickly hang up and get back to being happy with the family, damnit! You rotten ungrateful kids come back here and be loving right now! No, it wasn't that bad, but you felt like it when you were 10 or 12. When you're under 10 you think it's awesome because of all the food and people around and it was time to make up a show to put on after dinner! Then you become a moody pubescent for a while and everything sucks, then it gets fun again as you are of drinking age. The drinking age was 18 back then, I remember being allowed to start having a glass of wine around 16 at holiday meals. Good times. Again, different world. I never understood why sitting around the adult table after the food was all gone and drinking wine and laughing hysterically was so interesting that no one wanted to see our little kid show... until I became eligible to sit at the adult table. I enjoy those times with family immensely.

However, don't think I'm one of these people that wear a snippy button that says "You can wish me a Merry Christmas", or bitterly proclaim to be a victim of the "War on Christmas". Oh stop being a victim, would ya'? So it's not as sacred as it used to be, sad but true. Get over it. Yes, some people take the "Let's be all inclusive and just wish everyone Happy Holidays as to not rock the boat" thing too far. And yes, some people were just trying to make everyone happy but just pull up your big girl panties and take what anyone gives you, be it a Merry Christmas or Happy Holidays, and give whatever you want back whether it be Merry Christmas, Happy Holidays, Happy Festivus, Happy Hanukkah, or Happy Kwanzaa. Getting all bent out of shape about it, kind of defeats the spirit of the season, doesn't it?

Getting mad at others for their war on your holiday, kind of makes you look silly and not very religious-like. We've become an awful group of entitled people, don't you think? And it's on all sides, don't get me wrong. Shame on the people who insist you respect their beliefs and NOT wish them a specific holiday and instead must give a generic "Happy Holidays", and shame on the people who insist you respect their beliefs and wish them their appropriate holiday greeting. Hello?! Did you notice a recurring theme

10

there? I say just feel lucky someone said hello and wished you a happy something!

I get it, I get it, there are some corporate or government entities that have made waves with the "stay generic" for the holidays mandate. This city puts up a nativity scene, that person says "You offend me" with your scene of a kid laying in hay being sniffed by a camel because it represents Christianity, a specific religion which contradicts the ole separation of Church and State thing. I get it. That corporation says "No Christmas trees in our store and just say Happy Holidays", and this person says "Hey I can say Merry Christmas if I want to!" I get that too. It's all misguided and for someone to think it's all some vast conspiratorial plot to undermine Christianity, well... I think it's time to up your meds. Getting mad is counter-productive. In my book, at least. I would be remiss to perpetuate the cycle by getting mad at you for getting mad at them... and so on, and so on.

Think of it this way... say you are a non-Christian and you go through the checkout line and the clerk wishes you a "Merry Christmas". Do you think there was much thought put into it other than, I hope you enjoy the day or time of year? If you are non-Christian, will you grab them by the collar and yell, "I'm not about that Christmas %$#@!"? No because you'll make poor McKenzie making $8.00 an hour after school, cry. Wish 'em whatever you want back then! Say "Happy Holidays", "Happy Hanukkah", or "Happy Vulcan Feast Day" if you want. It's the sentiment, not the literalization of it.

Yes, this missive seems like a contradiction as I reminisced about keeping things sacred but wanting people to lighten up in staying strict about their holiday. But it was just that, it was indeed just reminiscing. It's not the same. It's a different world. However, you can still celebrate things in the manner you wish and that doesn't require being a jerk to others. We start calling for heads to roll and adhere to strict religious beliefs, sooner or later we'll be stoning women for showing their hair, or sending people away on rail cars never to be seen again. Seems a bit extreme? Yes, no, maybe. But that's sometimes the direction things go as people try to force their beliefs on others, it sometimes gets carried away. I don't mean that to be a paranoid theory to induce mass-hysteria, I just meant it as well, take a look at history.

Just wish each other well in the manner you are comfortable and accept that from others as well. Vive la difference is what I say. From me, Merry Christmas... but you all enjoy whatever you like now, ya' hear?

3 NEW YEAR, NEW PURGE

It's a new year... I bet you didn't know that, huh? Yes yes, and you are being bombarded with New Year's Day kitsch and people telling you what you should do for the New Year. New Year's Day sales... "Buy this!" "Buy that!" Make resolutions! Lose weight now! Well, here's my two cents. I don't want you to buy anything. Really, please don't buy a thing. I do want you to lose something though. No, it's not weight, unless of course you really want to, then knock yourself out. I do want you to lose junk, baggage, grudges, clutter, bad people and bad vibes. 'Tis the season to purge, eradicate, eliminate, liquidate, exfoliate, expunge, sluice, slough and molt.

I've recently experienced that throwing crap away has done me a world of good. Cleansed my soul even. It's funny because it first came to me almost two years ago. I was moving and I thought it's really time to get rid of some of this stuff. Ya' know, broken or beat up furniture, my 15 year old mattress, my son's 18 year old mattress, stuff that didn't fit, ugly Christmas tablecloths garnered in a Secret Santa exchange that I hadn't ever used in 10 years... Then about six months after that I got a little bolder. I don't know what got into me; it came on like a sudden gust of wind from the Staten Island dump that jolted my senses. I decided it was time to get rid of the old furniture.

When I moved, I moved temporarily into my boyfriend's house. He has a four bedroom house packed to the gills so there was no room for anything of mine, so I put it in storage. I went into the unit one day and needed to shift stuff around to get to things and it was really tight and I said to myself, "Self, that couch and loveseat have got to go". Now, since my divorce 14 years ago I've been incredibly cheap. I have hung onto crap because I knew I could never afford another one of it. Especially furniture. I lost jobs, my ex didn't pay child support, it was always one thing or another causing me to teeter from side to side of the poverty line. Anyway, I couldn't afford to replace things.

But I started to do better financially and I thought, by the time I move into a new place I can afford it. Even if I can't, we'll sit on the floor, I need to do this. I got rid of the couch and loveseat that I got in 1997 while we were married. OUR furniture, marital property. It was good Ethan Allen furniture but it had been through three kids from infancy to teen-dom spilling various things on it and having fannies with leaky diapers sitting on it. It had also been through two dogs, a cat, and an incontinent adult (which was probably the worst offense). I was even using a slip cover but who was I kidding? It looked like I was living in a College Heights apartment, and there should be an empty keg in the corner and a bong under the couch.

It felt good, a little scary but good. But I needed to stop worrying. Some have a theory that to make room for new things you need to get rid of old things, clear a space for the Universe to bring you good things. I believe if I continue to work hard and focus on the future, what I need, will come. Oh by no means do I think it's magic. But I do believe in the power of will, intention, and asking the universe. No, I don't own a 16 disc set from some self-help guru, I just intuitively believe in... let's call it the power of positive thinking.

Then I hit the closets and drawers. You know all those pants and dresses that you've been hanging onto for ten years because if you "just lose ten pounds" you can fit in them? Well guess what they aren't even in style anymore. Get. Rid. Of. Them! I did. Stuff I hadn't worn in years thinking it might come in handy someday... gone. I even found missives to and from my ex-husband, and an old boyfriend's (very bad, very toxic old boyfriend) phone numbers... threw all them out. I even found old lingerie from relationships past, what the hell was I gonna' use that for again, it didn't even fit? Gone.
I've also decided to stop answering texts, emails, Facebook posts, Tweets, and so on from people that are just no good for me. You know that guy that you were nuts about but just manages to get under your skin and makes you angry but you just can't manage to stay away? I just said no, finally. So should you.

I also did another interesting thing. It seems I was hanging onto a few hurts, grudges, and failures. Yes, failures. I didn't think that was possible but I was. I didn't realize I was doing it. All my failures kept running on an endless loop in my head and every time a new one happened I'd chalk it up to "That's just me and my crappy life". I was a 5'2" redheaded version of Eeyore. What I didn't realize is I was perpetuating the failures, bad luck, whatever you want to call it. Even some of the "failures" I was hanging onto weren't even real failures! They were stories that I told myself were failures.

So I did a great exercise. First I wrote down each thing I thought was a failure, I addressed it, acknowledged it happened, told myself to snap out of it if it wasn't a real thing, then I told myself what I had learned from that experience and how it actually had a valuable lesson. Then, I envisioned a basket filled with little orbs, each one was labeled with one of those failures. I had all of my perceived failures in a basket and I pictured standing on the shore of an ocean. I took out the orbs one by one, said goodbye and threw them into the ocean and pictured them exploding on impact and dissolving into the sea. That was so I couldn't dive down to the bottom of the water later and retrieve them, know what I'm sayin'?

I felt an enormous weight lift off me. I feel healthier, cleaner, more positive, more whole. You should try it too. To start off a great 2015... just get rid of your literal and figurative junk.

4 NOT EVERYONE WANTS YOUR ADVICE

You know that old chestnut from Voltaire, "Opinion has caused more trouble on this little earth than plagues or earthquakes"? You're probably more familiar with the saying, "Opinions are like a#$ holes, everyone has one"? Well I have a new take on this quote, "Opinions are like fruit, some are good, some are bad, you don't know until you squeeze them." Wow, that was really kind of lame, wasn't it? Anyway...

I've had to face many tough decisions in the past couple of years. You know a lot of "crossroads in life" type of stuff. As I've had to make some decisions about my career, finances, living situation, kid's college futures, my parent's health, etc...everyone has something different to say, advice or opinion to offer. And most often it's the complete opposite of what the last person said. If the opinions were charted they'd looked like the echocardiogram of a speed freak.

Oh don't get me wrong, advice is good. Bouncing things off people is good. We all need to weigh things out. But if you hear from too many people, solicited or unsolicited, if you're weighing them and it starts to feel like one of those people from a TLC documentary like "The 900 lb Man" sitting on your chest… wait maybe the 900 lb man riding Mothra… well then it's time to stop bouncing things off others. As my mother used to say, "Too many cooks spoil the soup."

One of the most intelligent things my ex-husband ever said as I obsessed daily with the "What to Expect When You're Expecting" books when I was pregnant was, "Throw the damn book away!" "Throw all the books away" (OK maybe save one for reference). Yea, he was right. I kept reading all these different opinions and doubting my ability to make rational decisions. I worked myself up more than a bag of cats tossed down a hill. I was worrying and second guessing non-stop. Oh yes, I think they call it "anxiety".

When you begin to doubt your own compass is when you need to take a step back. For instance, I have my second child in the college selection process right now. She is a senior at Our Lady of Mercy High School; we did the whole investigating thing—campus visits and mailing applications. And now we wait. She's had a few acceptances come in; waiting for more and then financial aid packages will be the deciding factor. I'm not a Rockefeller after all.

Now my son is currently a junior at one of the most expensive colleges in the universe, NYU. I'm trying to be realistic with my daughter. He got scholarships but will still have a few big loans and the travel expense back and forth adds up. I allowed my daughter to apply to her dream schools but we need to weigh things out before accepting.

Fortunately this child had very reasonable dream schools. But if I can't afford to bring you home for Thanksgiving, we have a problem. I have some people insisting I send my next two children to state schools or community college for two years then four year state school. Um no, you don't know all the facts of my situation.

Nothing against them but state schools really aren't any cheaper in my circumstance (single mom) because they don't give as much aid as private schools do. I just know my kids, I know how they are and they wouldn't be happy living at home and going to community college. There isn't anything wrong with community college, it's wonderful. It's just a different atmosphere. For example...I started out at a small college in Pennsylvania my freshman year and was miserable, then sophomore year I transferred. I transferred to a much bigger school in New England and I was as happy as a clam. It was about the whole atmosphere. My grades got better too. For some kids, it doesn't really matter, others it does. Some people will just go anywhere because a degree is a degree. Others look for the whole college experience. And that is the beauty of life... to each his own.

"Your kids should do this". "Your kids should do that". "Your kids would be happier doing..." "It would be best if you did..." "Trust me, I know".

Holy moly, stop telling me what to do! Argh! I've raised these kids for 21 years pretty much on my own and have gotten this far, do you think I'm stupid?

Don't answer that. The thing is, I'm the one that lives my life day to day. I'm the one who has all the inside info. And even if I'm not 100% sure of what to do, I'm a risk taker. I'll give it the old college try (no pun intended) and see what happens. Let the chips fall where they may. I'm not like the people who say "What if?" "What if?" 'What if?" I'm a "Let's try it and if we need to change our course, we will" kind of gal. Maybe that wasn't always the best thing, but at least I didn't do it with anything crazy like, "Let's try heroin and just see what happens" or "Let's just try unprotected sex with this guy who injects meth and see what happens" (I don't know, is injecting meth even a thing?).

If you are obsessed with making a move on the condition that you can predict the outcome, then you can become paralyzed. Conversely if you leap without thinking, you can find yourself in a heap load of trouble. I say weigh things out, then take an educated leap of faith. And there's a lot to be said for gut instinct. (Unless of course you're a rapist, murderer, or pedophile) I'm not afraid. But once I've made up my mind... leave me the heck alone. I don't mean to be mean, I know some people are just trying to help but sometimes advice comes out as "I know better than you do" especially if you are insistent. That's rude. The outcome will eventually be apparent to me; I don't need your predictive "Mark my words..." shenanigans, because you really don't know. No one knows.

5 WHAT'S WITH ALL THE SOCIAL MEDIA HATE?

I love to interact with people. I love to socialize. I love to joke around. My favorite thing to do in the world is laugh. And I love social media to interact with people... well I used to. I don't even want to look at it anymore, it's so depressing. There is so much negativity; it changes my mood within 30 seconds of looking at my Facebook feed. What's with all the hatred?

I don't mind a little complaining, irritation, annoyance, even anger, but be reasonable for God's sake. There is just so much out and out seething hate combined with broad generalizations and ridiculous accusations that it literally leaves me shaking my head as I turn off the computer. Sometimes my jaw drops at what some people I know actually believe.

Take for instance, politics. Yea, we know that one is usually the biggest offender. But it really gets me when people can't refrain from using an expletive every time they mention our President or some other government official. Ok, we get it you don't like the person because of their beliefs, political party, gender, or race, but let it go already. Hanging on to all that anger all day, every day is a complete waste of energy. You know what else it means? That person wins. Yup, they got under your skin, they got your attention. Ha ha! Does that make you even angrier? Well, then at this point I think you need anger management... or meds.

Oh and yes I did say you might not like them because of their race or gender. Face it, some of us all have deep-seeded issues or just involuntary reactions that make us prejudice. We learned it somewhere. I don't believe people are born with hate in their heart, I think it is cultivated by our environment. People in your world teach you things— maybe your family or friends or teachers or even TV. Somebody had to plant the seed. Unless of course you are a sociopath or something, even then I think that's more that you have no regard for other people's feelings or welfare rather than hate. But combine that with some trigger and you've got hate. I better go check my DSM-IV Codes on what mental health issues include anger.

Anyway, the things that people post about other people or issues that are so far removed from them that they are so angry about is completely beyond me. I often feel, the items they are raging against are either an outlet for anger they have inside from something completely unrelated or they are choosing to focus on that as a distraction. Like um, hey dude why don't you focus on your juvenile delinquent kid at home rather than the President saluting with a coffee cup or the "freeloaders" on welfare? I'm not saying you shouldn't focus on the big picture; yes we need to worry about our world but raging anger about anything near or far is pretty useless.

The other thing that bothers me is that most of the statements are completely misguided, untrue, or spoken by a person that has no personal knowledge of the subject whatsoever. Remember that old chestnut that the bible gave us? "Judge not, lest he be judged?" If you haven't lived it, you can't assume that you know whereof you speak. You don't know thing one about the homeless stranger you see on the street, but you'll go telling tales that you "know" that "All those people do is drink and steal and they're crazy." Did you talk to the person? No? Did you follow them all day to see what they do? No? Did you do a background check on them? No? Well then don't make sweeping hateful generalizations about them. And it's simple math, even if one person in a group of 100 is honest and 99 of that group are dishonest, it still does not equate to ALL of those people are dishonest. Get it?

It's one thing if you have a thought on a subject like, "I wonder how many people that are on welfare have been on it long term and seem to make it a lifestyle? What can we do to break that cycle?" That's thoughtful and proactive. Saying "All people on welfare are lazy deadbeat losers" is, well... just hateful. What if somebody posted something that applied to you, like all people that lived in your area were a*@holes? And most likely by someone that has never ever lived in your area or doesn't personally know anyone that has lived in your area? Chew on that for a minute.

I have a theory according to a lot of psychology I studied in college that a lot of anger is based on the need to be right or not be vulnerable, which is ruled by what... our ego, right? So anger is fueled by ego. It's also fueled by fear... the fear of being vulnerable. What is with a person's overwhelming need to be "right" or "not taken advantage of"? It's another waste of valuable energy. I know because I used to be like that. After my divorce, I was so determined to never be duped or controlled again that I became very defensive, paranoid, and just plain shrew-like. You see my ex-husband was a bit of a controller, verbally abusive, and ended up having an affair on me while I was pregnant with our third child. After all the hurt and anger, I really felt humiliated that I let that all happen to me. And what's that? Ego.

So post-divorce, as I started to date I became very, um... accusatory. A guy didn't call, I'd be all like "I know what you're doing, you're blowing me off, at least have the balls to say it to my face!" And uh, well turns out he just had a kid that needed to go to the emergency room after his little league game. *Ahem* Yea, I did a whole lot of that. And that's what people do on social media... "Our government will not humiliate me with their conspiracies to control me and let big business make money off me!" Why? Why are you so obsessed with that? Is it all because you can say, "I told you so?" So, you can be "right"? Oh hello, your ego just called, it made a reservation for one for your entire being.

The best thing I ever did was learn to be vulnerable and learn to "accept" things, that doesn't mean I'm not still cautious of being hurt or wronged but now I just look for the signs and then quietly walk away. Accepting things is awesome. I had suffered from anxiety most of my early life. I had a huge fear of death, especially at night. It was like the perfect anxiety cocktail, all the stuff you're afraid of blends together as you try to go to sleep. After years of therapy and meds, I arrived at the fact that... we're all gonna' die someday. And I also learned I was just afraid of the unknown. Once I became older and experienced more natural death (you know old relatives dying off and whatnot) I realized that it is just a part of life and it actually is a weird beautiful peaceful experience. I can't explain that one, but I know I became less afraid.

That's why I don't feel the need to arm myself to the tee at home or wherever I go, because I am NOT afraid. Those who are afraid build up arsenals. Those who aren't are willing to battle what comes their way with what they have and will have the courage to know when there is absolutely nothing they can do about something. I'm not saying to give up, but just know when to walk away or focus attention elsewhere. Did you ever notice that when a terminally ill person decides "I'm ready to go" that an odd peaceful calm comes over them? It's not a coincidence.

I can't change other people. I can do what needs to be done, say if they did something criminal to me I'd report them and let the chips fall where they may. Otherwise I just cut them out of my life. I won't waste my breath ranting and raving waiting for justice or for them to make amends and say "I'm sorry". Not gonna' happen. Sometimes you just can't get blood from a stone and you need to let it go. So folks on Facebook ranting and raving, either do something constructive to try and help, or quit your bitching and let it go. Then do something really useful like hug your family or friends.

6 THINGS THAT JUST DON'T MAKE SENSE TO ME

Lately I've been thinking a lot about people and how all of our thoughts can be so vastly different. How can all of our perceptions, tastes, and values all vary so greatly?

Ok there are the basic differences in a person's character. You know the old good vs. evil. What makes one person Mother Theresa and another person Adolph Hitler? Where did they go wrong? Where did they go right? People even have differences of opinion on what is right or wrong. That leads me to the ever complex issue of common sense. What is common sense? Some people have it, some people don't. Some people think they have it but their idea of common sense is vastly different from others. For instance, some people believe it is common sense to back into a parking space in a parking lot, so they can get out easier. Others think that defies common sense, since you are holding up a long line of cars in the parking lot as you try to back into your spot.

See?! See what I mean?! It's little things like that! It's driving me mad I tell ya', mad! For instance I have a long list of things that don't make any sense to me and actually the opposite of the thing that seems just like common sense to me. Shall we take a look? Okay, then...

1. Wearing pantyhose/stockings with open toed shoes. What the hell? You might as well wear socks, then! The point of opened toed shoes is to see... your toes! Nobody wants to see your seemingly webbed toes with a big seam running across the top. Don't even get me started if you're wearing the reinforced toe kind. Lord, just go check yourself into the nearest nursing home if you're doing that. The trend is to just simply not wear pantyhose anymore, but if you must, wear closed toe shoes.

2. Driving in the left lane for an indefinite period of time on a highway. The left lane is for passing! Did you not read the manual in driver ed or perhaps that was the question you got wrong on the written portion of your driver test? Maybe you just missed the gigantic sign that says, "Slower Traffic Keep Right"? Oh was that too difficult to understand? Ya' see, you stay to the right unless you come up behind somebody in front of you who is travelling at a slower rate of speed and then you pass them in the left lane. It doesn't mean that maybe you fashion yourself a lively, nimble driver and you deserve a special slot in the left lane indefinitely. No! Passing only! And move back to the right when you're done.

3. Not standing on top of someone in the checkout line. It's called personal space... obey it! I have my business to conduct, I'm puttin' my Shopper's Club

card in and all that, waiting for my total, you back the heck off me until I'm done. You clipping the back of my heels with your shopping car isn't going to make the cashier check me out any faster. And don't worry, no one else is going to jump ahead of you in line and take your place... they couldn't possibly, as you haven't even afforded enough room for even the Holy Spirit to get between you and me. If I can tell what kind of detergent you've washed your clothes in then you're too damn close!

4. Yelling at people, particularly screaming. What is the point? I get it, sometimes we are in the moment and we're a bit exasperated and you blurt something out. It happens a lot when I'm driving alone. (Whoopsie, my bad) But to have an argument where two people are screaming at each other, you're just making noise, it's nothing productive, and no one is hearing anyone's debate points. And it just looks silly. I think some people think it's like verbal arm wrestling, "I'm going to yell so loud over your yelling that you will just give up or go hoarse before I do". Especially yelling at your child, I always thought my Mother was a lunatic when she yelled at me. I didn't respect that (sorry, Mom) and I didn't usually hear her point because I was so busy rolling my eyes in my head and thinking how embarrassing she was, I didn't even listen to what she was saying. Again, sorry Mom, I know you're not on Earth anymore but I know you are still reading this. Think about it, when someone is yelling at you do you think, "Oh yes I fully understand your argument in favor of not eating genetically modified organisms as you are screaming at me"?

5. Driving around with your handicap permit hanging from your rearview mirror. How can you see?! It's not

like it's some little tag, it's a huge card the size of a pamphlet. I'm thinking if you already have some sort of disability, you don't want your driving further hampered by this big piece of cardstock obstructing your view! Furthermore I don't think people need to know that you are handicapped while you are driving, only when you're parked. Unless of course you are such a horrendous driver, you want all to know and feel bad and give you a break.

Again, this is MY reality. These are my beliefs. Yours may be completely different. I respect that. I guess. Kind of. Unless they don't make any sense whatsoever or are illegal. I guess my main point is it just baffles me how we can all think so differently. I'm not saying, you should all think like me... that would be a scary, scary world if you all did. My point is that I'm curious as to what are the things that lead people to think so differently, or perceive things so differently? Environment, upbringing, IQ, religion? It all adds up. Variety is the spice of life. Everyone being different is a beautiful thing. But it won't stop me from lying awake at night wondering why pantyhose are still sold. *wink*

7 MADGE'S ODE TO MEN

This being our men's issue, I've decided to write about... men. Hey, can't live with 'em, can't live without 'em... am I right, ladies? Let's face it, men are important. Without them the human race would cease to propagate.

I also wanted to write about men because I was once called a "man hater" by a male blogger. I've blocked him on several social media sites after years of him popping up everywhere I was on the internet and calling me a "man hater". All because about eight years ago, he wrote a blog about how much all the women of Rochester suck and I defended us (the women of Rochester) in a comment. I simply said we are awesome women, and suggested that perhaps he was the problem. This prompted his years-long grudge and stalking.

I definitely do not hate men. I do not blame all men every time I have a disappointing experience with one. That would just be stupid. I have a son, whom I love more than life itself. I'm even friendly/civil with my ex-husband whom I have plenty of reasons not to be. Unfortunately my Dad passed away two years ago, but I did (and still do) love him like crazy.

It's very common to see odes to women, like we don't get enough props so somebody has to write a Hallmark card about us to remember the good that we do instead of just judging us by our weight or age or appearance. Men have been running the world for centuries, so they really don't need any more fuel for their fire. But so no one thinks I'm a man hater, I am going to give them their just adulation.

Often times women will speak of men in feminist terms. Yes, those of us in the Baby Boom and younger age group (ages 65 to newborn) have been raised in a world where women can and are expected to "do it all". We have the mindset of being equal. Well, that we are supposed to be, even though some areas of life haven't caught up to that. We are no longer taught that our life goal is to find a good man to take care of us. We no longer feel the only point in going to college is to get an MRS degree, but we can actually get an education and make something of ourselves. Some of us have been taught that men are a nice complement to our lives, others who have been raised by an angrier pack of feminists think you don't need one at all.

At the moment for me, a man is not a necessity in traditional terms. I own my own house, I have a job, I have insurance, I am handling raising my children with aplomb. However... men are nice. I am heterosexual after all and enjoy the company of men because I am attracted to them. Certain needs are just in your DNA and hard to avoid. Here are reasons why I like men...

Hugs from friends are nice but there's nothing like having a nice smelling man's arms wrapped around you. (Yea, bad smelling kind of ruins it, although sometimes the slight musky smell of sweat equity is a little intoxicating) As strong as I proclaim I am, I confess I enjoy the arms of a man that make me feel safe and secure, if even for a moment. Just like I enjoyed the security of the arms of my Mom and Dad when they were alive.

As hard as we try, men can still bring a certain swagger that we can't. Sorry, no hoodlum will quiver if I try to stop him from mistreating someone else, but if a confident male stands up to him, they have better chances. Unless of course hoodlum has a shiv and confident guy doesn't. And I'm not gonna' lie, sometimes I wish I had a guy with a bat to send outside to investigate a strange noise instead of me just randomly yelling out the window, "You better get out of here before I call the police!"

Try as I might, I can't lift that 100lb bag of whatever. (I can still lift a 50lb bag, see that's the feminist in me) Oh I'm sure I could find a female weightlifter to do it but I could find a healthy male to do it a lot faster. I could totally swing a dead cat and find a dude that could lift it. It might take me a string of dead cats tied together to make a 50 mile radius to find a woman that could do it.

And the obvious... we need men to procreate. Even if you don't physically insert Part A into Part B, you still need their necessary ingredients to make a new human being. Having three children of my own, I understand this. Even if for recreational purposes, unless you're a lesbian, most women enjoy the process even without the new human outcome. Ahem. Am I being vague enough? Heterosexual women have a need for men either to procreate or to satisfy desires. Lesbian women don't need men to fulfill desires but they still need them if they would like a child, even if to just make an anonymous donation at a reputable facility. However having a nice male role model somehow, somewhere in a child's life (could be friend, teacher, uncle) is always beneficial. If only to have the viewpoint of both genders.

Men are funny, strong, smart, beautiful, caring, loving, and on average make more money than women. I say this to get a laugh but unfortunately it's true. And as I said "on average". Don't get your panties in a bunch wealthy working ladies. However chances are, if your company (unless you own it) hired a man to do your same job, he'd make more money. Can't explain why that still happens in this day and age but it does. But back to the nice men... We love you and we still need you. You are not obsolete, we still want you around. As many jokes as we make, we still adore you. Some of my best friends are men! (You know that old cliché') But it's true, I enjoy the company of men, I love them and the world would be a sad (and much less populated) place without them. Show some love, hug a man today.

8 LADIES! TAKE THE TIME TO TAKE CARE OF YOUR HEALTH!

It's a well-known fact that women are usually quick to take care of others before themselves. Often times in a house where there is a mother and children and possibly various other family members (father, grandparents, house guests), the mother or matriarch of the house will make sure everyone else's health is taken care of but rarely takes care of herself, and if she does at all, it's last.

Some women just enjoy being martyrs... come on, be honest, you know a few. But most just honestly have the natural nurturing demeanor where others come first. So ladies... let's stop that. Well, I don't mean stop being nurturing, I mean let's not neglect our own health. And stop being martyrs too, that's annoying.

I'm not just talking about physical health either, mental health too. But let's take a look at physical health first. If you have an ache or a pain, please see the doctor. Don't do the typical, "Oh it will just go away tomorrow". If in fact you wake up the next day and the ache or pain is still there, go see the doctor. It could be the difference between finding something serious in the early stages or finding something serious when it's too late. No mother is any good to her children if she is deceased. No really, I'm serious.

But let's not wait for aches and pains to come up, let's go for annual physicals as well. That includes both a regular physical by your primary care doctor and an exam by your OB/GYN. No they are not the most pleasant of experiences but I could think of worse things. Seriously, like you know, giving birth. That was far more painful and time consuming than a pelvic exam. And running a marathon... that's far more painful and time consuming as well. Getting hit by a bus, that would suck too. I'd take the pelvic exam all day long over a marathon or bus. Well, ok maybe not all day long, that's a little excessive.

Going to the doctor is not the only way to ensure health, it starts at home. Make sure to get plenty of rest, that means go to bed and sleep rather than staying up until 12am to polish the silverware or mop the floor. That stuff will keep until the next day. Unless the Queen of England is coming to visit, nobody cares what chores have been done.

Also eat healthy and exercise. Eating healthy does not mean eating a cupcake you grabbed off the counter for dinner while you drive a kid to hockey practice. Yes, yes I know I've dined on such delicacies myself. Sometimes you have to do what you have to do but if you try to eat something better when you get home later, that's helpful. And by better I mean some fruits and vegetables, not cereal. Try to remember the "Strive for Five" principle, try to get at least five servings of fruits and vegetables a day. Hey, one serving is an accomplishment for a lot of us. One is better than none.

Exercise. Believe it or not, there is exercise that involves more than carrying baskets of laundry up and down two flights of stairs or carrying children around. Yes, that can be quite tiring and strenuous but it's helpful to get at least 20 minutes of continuous exercise like walking, aerobics, or riding to give your heart and muscles a good workout. Not to mention, going out for a walk or run is great to spend time alone and clear your mind. Or going to the gym helps you to clear your head... or find a hot date if you're single.

Which brings me to... mental health. Mental health is just as important as physical health. We women need to make it a priority to take care of our mental health. Think of it this way, it could save your children or spouse's life. A woman gets stressed out and just stuffs it down and down and down until the pressure builds and her head explodes and the blast takes out the entire neighborhood. Nobody wants that. In all seriousness, taking care of your mental health can prevent poor physical health and strains in relationships with family and friends.

Not only is general mental health essential but taking care of your soul is a wise idea too. No, it's not the same as mental health. I mean, it's close, it's internal but it's... different. Your soul is your inner peace, your hopes and dreams, your love of others and life, your motivation, your inspiration, your core. I know you didn't think I was one of those flaky spiritual types, did ya'? Well, this month I turn 50, yea you heard me.

And it's taken me 50 years to learn that taking care of your soul is essential to one's well-being. It's important to have hopes and dreams and peace within. I can't explain it but write down your hopes and dreams and see how you feel then try a meditation exercise. Seriously it's like a power wash of your brain, you can focus better.

So there you have it ladies, take it from me, I've been to hell and back and over the river and through the woods. I used to think I could power my way through anything but even the strongest of women can't do it by sheer willpower alone. Five years ago my world was falling apart, no job, about to lose my home and I ended up in the hospital thinking I was having a heart attack. I couldn't eat or sleep or create a moment's peace. Luckily it was only an anxiety attack but it made me realize I had to stop panicking, literally. Taking five minutes to eat and then go in my room by myself and shut the door for 15 minutes pretty much saved my life. Running around like Chicken Little trying to save my kids and the world nearly gave me a heart attack. I think the anxiety attack was actually a warning shot fired by God.

You don't want to leave your kids motherless, do you? You don't want to leave your mate alone and sad, do you? Most important of all, you need to be healthy for you. Life is a wonderful, beautiful journey... don't miss it.

9 DINING ETIQUETTE IS A LOST ART... MADGE TO THE RESCUE!

It's always so wonderful to talk about food and wine and how delicious they are and fun to make (not for me), but some important items always seem to be left out when we discuss these things... how to act when you're eating and drinking with other people. Whether it's company at your house or dining at a restaurant, most people seriously need an etiquette refresher. Madge to the rescue...

Let's get down to brass tacks, shall we? Here are some things that my mother taught me and to this day I am still a stickler about. I'm always harping on my poor kids about this stuff, well actually I don't have to anymore because they already have these things engrained in them. Gotta' start 'em early...

1. If you have been invited to someone's house for dinner... NEVER go empty handed! Ugh, so rude. It's like showing up and saying, "OK, I'm here, feed me!" No, you have to contribute something to the evening –

a bottle of wine, flowers, a desert. Or at the very least, something to just say thank you.

2. When sitting down to dinner at either a friend's house, a restaurant, or even your own home... gentleman, remove your hat. It's just a sign of respect. I don't know why, I know there's a reason, just do it.

3. Gentleman, pull out a ladies chair, even if you don't, at least wait until she sits first. Trust me it will score you big points... big points.

4. Put the phones away. You're there to break bread and enjoy each other's company, do it. It's rude to ignore each other because you're texting everyone to see where you're meeting up later. But it's also rude to hold up the ordering because you have to take 18 pictures of the group or selfies because your hair wasn't just right in the first 17 pics. You're keeping the server from moving along the flow of the restaurant and holding up others in your party who actually want to eat. Also, all the picture taking looks incredibly self-absorbed to the other patrons. Tacky.

5. At a restaurant, don't tell others what to order. Like, don't tell your date, "I can't decide between the fish and the beef, so why don't you get the fish so I can have a taste of yours and I'll get the beef". Um no. What, so you can eat half of my food? No thanks, I'll order what I want, and eat all of it.

6. And another on the ordering note, don't get on another person's case about what they're ordering. For instance, if you're a vegan and someone at the table orders meat, don't be a jerk and go off on them about how the animals are tortured and shame them

into being a herbivore. That is not the place or time.
Or telling someone that what they're ordering is not
the healthiest choice, like deep fried chocolate cake,
smothered in high fat cheese... a lecture in "healthy
food choices" is not appropriate at the time. You just
look like a self-righteous jerk. "Food shaming" is
never a good idea.

7. In support of all our brothers and sisters who give
their lives to serving others... in restaurants... don't be
a putz to the server or bus boy. They are not your
servant or slave, they are people doing a job. Yes,
there are a few with attitude, but if you fight back with
attitude it just makes it a miserable dining experience
for everyone around you. Most of the time if there is a
problem, like food taking too long or food being
cooked wrong, it's not the servers fault. Don't try and
take a pound of flesh out of the messenger.

8. A big pet peeve here... for the love of God wait until
everyone gets their food before you start shoveling
yours in your mouth! The waiter is bringing out the
plates, he sets yours down, Betty's down, and Fred's
down... Ethel, Lucy, and Barney are still waiting on
theirs's and you start digging in. How rude! Ethel,
Lucy, and Barney are still waiting and salivating as
you chow down on your Salisbury steak in front of
them. Same thing in a home, they're still passing the
potatoes around for God's sake and you're already
elbows deep in tuna casserole! Knock it off! Wait until
everyone has a full plate in front of them, and... go!

9....And when you get said food, don't shovel. There is
no need to eat like you haven't seen a meal since the
Clinton Administration. Eat slowly, in small amounts
on your fork/spoon. You don't need to get down to

plate level and push food into your gullet like it's a truck full of hot tar onto a driveway.

10. This should go without saying... don't talk with your mouth full. (See what I did there?) No, really, it's disgusting. Nothing you have to say is that important that it can't wait until your teeth have ground down your food into digestible bites and broken it down by enzymes in your saliva and sent down into your tummy.

11. You may think you're a big shot if you send food back because it's "Not to your liking", but it's rude to the staff and chef and uncomfortable for everyone else at the table. And then if they are nice people they will feel compelled to stop eating until you get your food back and it's just an awkward situation. Of course you can send it back if something is raw and could get you sick, or burnt to a crisp and tastes like charcoal. And I guess possibly if you take a bite and you realize it contains an ingredient that you are allergic to or makes you violently ill. "Coriander?! I didn't know this had coriander in it, I'll be in the bathroom for a week!" And if you do have to send something back, be polite and diplomatic. If you are rude or nasty, you're food might come back with unknown and unwanted human by-product ingredients added to it.

12. Whenever, you need to leave the table, excuse yourself. Say, "Excuse me, I need to go to the ladies' room" Please don't say, "I gotta' pee." Ugh, that's so crass and classless.

13. At the end of the meal, be a good tipper. Remember, servers make less than minimum wage and depend on your tips to make a living. If the

service was really that bad, leave a lower tip but still within the 15-20% range. Ok if it's really really bad do 10%, but never something rude like leaving one penny or a glib note on the charge slip. If the service was that bad, report it to the manager and let them handle it.

I could probably go on and on but I'll refrain. I don't want to re-write Emily Post. But I do think dining etiquette is a lost art that we all need to re-visit. General civility is a lost art. Maybe if we take a deep breath and show these subtle signs of respect to each other and respect the idea of the sit-down meal, we might all feel a little more peaceful. And we'd have a lot less annoying selfies and pictures of food on Facebook. Bon appetite!

10 DON'T TELL ME WHAT TO WEAR

"Fashion, turn to the left. Fashion, turn to the right. Ooooh, fashion. We are the goon squad and we're coming to town. Beep beep. Beep beep." – David Bowie, "Fashion"

Girl, don't get me started. I love fashion. I love clothes. I love shoes. Creatively inspired fashion is best. What you wear is the outward reflection of your personality. You are what you wear. So, don't tell me what to wear.

Yes, you are what you wear... that is why I have a problem with the show "What Not to Wear" on TLC. Or rather, now it's reincarnation as "Love, Lust, or Run" on TLC. The original featured Stacy London and Clinton Kelly, ambushing a poorly chosen soul who was nominated by family and friends of what they thought was a dire need of a wardrobe makeover. The new show just has Stacy, and to add insult to injury she has random people on the street critiquing these women's outfits by saying they love it, lust it, or would run away from it. I think that's kind of mean, don't you?

I mean, yes some women did look a little scary in ill-fitting or unflattering things. And some were afraid to reveal their true selves by masquerading as a stripper or farm hand or fairy princess. But then again, I think some of these women do really feel like a stripper, a farm hand, or a fairy princess.

I've always been a big fan of individualism. I myself being a radical individualist, I've been through many incarnations. In high school in the late '70s and early '80s I was uber preppy. In college, I was super punk and new wave, complete with sides of my head shaved and spiky hair on top. After college, a preppy/punk combo. Then came marriage and motherhood in the 90's and it was pretty much preppy mommy wear. In the last 15 years since my divorce, I would call myself hip, edgy, retro, alternative, country club broad. It depends on the day and my mood, really. Lately, I've been in a pinup style mood, or as I just generally call retro.

Of course, I try to wear things that are flattering to my figure. Read: look less fat. I am a fan of people flattering their figure. I will give that to the "What Not to Wear" people, they teach women how to wear items that fit. But I don't know, I just think if a chick wants to be a motorcycle mama or rockabilly gal, more power to her. Yea, there are some that look like clowns – too much makeup, really loud ill-fitting clothes. Nor am I a fan of a 55-year-old woman trying to look like a 20-year-old. There is always room for a little tweaking. But the show always makes these women out to be freaks. I say, "Screw you, Stacy. I think those gray streaks ala Bride of Frankenstein in your hair look really stupid. Whattaya' think about that?"

Ok, I feel better. But wait the other thing that makes me angry is that for the makeover, every woman comes out looking exactly the same! So to them, a satisfactory makeover is one where all women look like they just stepped out of Chico's or Banana Republic in a boring boxy, casual business look. Sure, you look great for a Sears catalog model, but not someone a guy would give a catcall to.

My 18-year-old daughter just made a great point when I asked about her thoughts on the show. She agreed that every woman looks exactly the same after the makeover and hates that. But she also said that there are some people that do need help with things like work attire. There were a few women who were frustrated because they wanted to be more successful in their careers, but they couldn't understand why it wasn't happening when they were dressed like a hooker or bag lady. Work and play clothes are often different, that's a given. There are certain jobs that require a certain... decorum, shall we say. I don't think I'd trust a doctor that wore a Speedo to work or an investment banker that dressed like an exotic dancer. Well, I mean I'm open minded but perhaps that person's superiors aren't. I have to admit there was one girl that I agreed needed a makeover. She was... I don't even know how to describe it. It was a combination of goth, Kabuki theater (white-face Japanese dancers), and Tim Burton movie character. Her face was an artist's canvas, falling just short of a Jackson Pollack painting. She was a hairdresser. I don't imagine many women would feel confident that she wouldn't make them look like a freak. The client's definition of a freak, that is.

I don't know, I think my involuntary sense of, "Don't tell me what to do!" leaps out of my chest whenever I see things like this. I enjoy people's differences. Variety is the spice of life. I'm sure also that they probably manufacture some of those story lines as if to portray a car wreck or freak show. I'm sure some uptight suburban Stepford Wife is like, "Oh yes, her Rosie the Riveter look is an abomination!" But I think it's almost kind of Mean Girls-ish. I can't stand to see people embarrassed or humiliated in front of others. That's more what I see this show as. But who am I to judge? I wouldn't be any better than those doing the judging on the show. But I do believe I'm a little more open-minded and kind when it comes to fashion... and people. Vive le difference!

11 NEVER CRUSH A CHILD'S DREAMS

When I was growing up, going to college was not optional... it was mandatory. My parents graduated from Penn State University in 1948 and 1949. I am the youngest of six children and all were college graduates or in college at the time when I was starting the college search process. No pressure, though.

Not only was college not optional but neither was going away to school. Living at home and going to college nearby was not an option. Damn, I had demanding parents! On one hand it was nice that my parents wanted us to go out and spread our wings, on the other hand it felt like "Get the hell out of my house!" (Which I know wasn't really the case but, yea...)

The other thing my parents were sticklers about, (if that weren't enough) was choosing a major. I'm not really sure what my brothers and sisters went through, to me their major selection process seemed pretty easy. They all seemed to know what they wanted to do for a living pretty early. I may be completely inaccurate, who knows. Oh don't get me wrong, I knew what I wanted to do my whole life. I knew from an early age. I'm talking from nursery school on, I knew what I wanted to do. However... it wasn't acceptable.

See, my parents were very practical, methodical, cautious people. You got a degree in something useful, something that would guarantee you a good living, and if it didn't guarantee a good living, it still had to be intellectually impressive. Who cares if there are not a lot of jobs requiring a degree in 17th Century Baroque Crockery, it sounds impressive.

So, I will never to this day forget the response when I was so excited to tell my parents that I had found some colleges I was interested in that had my major and I couldn't wait to get started. "Well, what would you like to study, Peg?" (That's what they called me then) I said, "I just love performing, I want to major in theater!" I was met with a blank stare, then a disapproving look, followed by my father saying, "I'm not paying for you to go to college to become a waitress".

My heart couldn't have sunk any lower. That was an upper cut to the chin combined with a vomit-inducing gut punch. (Figuratively speaking, my parents never beat me) That's what it felt like to my heart and soul, though. Obviously, since I still remember it vividly to this day. Oh, I've since forgiven my Dad for saying that, ya' know like just in my heart though, on accounta' him being deceased and all. But I made a vow... with all that is holy, I will never ever crush my kid's dreams or make their goals seem stupid.

I do understand where he was coming from, they wanted what was best for me and didn't want to see me struggle with not finding a job after I got out. Again with the practical thing. I get it, I want to see my kids earn a paycheck after they are done with college too. I don't want four years and hundreds of thousands of dollars to be all for naught. However, ya' know, the wording...

They did work on finding me an alternative. Since my father's brother had been in broadcasting, first radio then TV, since the 1930's, they suggested that might be close enough to theatre., and with the advent of cable TV, would be a lucrative business. I chose that thinking I could be the next great DJ or talk show host. Back then in the 80's you were either a news anchor or radio DJ, and the radio DJ's just played pre-programmed music that there was no deviation from and all you did was announce the title and artist. No room for my creativity. It wasn't like in the 70's where some cool musicophile FM DJ rambled on about the music. So after I got out into the working world, I was disappointed.

So, when it was time for my kids to start thinking college majors, I vowed I was going to be more... sensitive. I started by asking my kids what they love – areas of interest or specific subjects. Also I asked what jobs appealed to them. Then we discussed what subjects they did well in. From there we looked up vocations and what the current demand was in those industries and what the rate of pay was. Many of my friends and other parents feel the availability of jobs and pay rate in a certain field is the only way to choose a major. Any time a major choice is mentioned, their response is "Oh those don't make anything". Sorry, but I feel you have to love what you do. As a line in one of my all-time favorite movies Caddyshack goes, "Well the world needs ditch diggers too." Meaning, there is something for everyone and there is always a need for all types of jobs, even if they aren't the highest paying.

The key is to talk through it with your kids. Do research. Even have them go to certain places of business and shadow people who do things that they might find interesting. Colleges also offer plenty of opportunities to explore different areas of interests. For instance Rochester Institute of Technology annually offers an event for high school females to explore the fields of science and engineering. Make sure to check into it at your local colleges.

But first and foremost don't ever make your child feel like what they are interested in is "stupid". Here I am at 50 years old and I still vividly remember my parents telling me that acting, as a career was stupid. To a child, what you are interested in is what you are. If you tell them what they are interested in is stupid, they believe they are stupid. Please don't ever do that. Even if they say, "I'd like to be a stripper" or "I'm going to play in the NFL" or "I want to be a tight rope walker". No matter how disturbing, unrealistic, or silly it seems, just talk it through. Always encourage a child to believe in their dreams... and it has never ever hurt to think of a sure-fire money making back-up plan either.

12 YES, I DO LOVE MY BREASTS

In keeping with the October issue's Breast Cancer Awareness theme, I would like to discuss one very important item: breasts.

Now, in this day and age of clichés and platitudes about women not being represented by their bodies, but by their minds and hearts, most, in theory, will bristle at what I'm about to say. But it's just food for thought.

As women, our breasts are much of our identity. Just as any body part would be, it's yours, part of you. But breasts — just think about it. It starts when we are children. Little kids love to point out the fact that "girls have boobies and a vagina; boys have a penis."

So, when we get to puberty, breasts seem to become a focus for everybody. Girls are worried about keeping up with other girls and "getting them," while boys seem to be obsessed with girls who do have them and terribly cruel to girls who don't. Oh yes, you remember all the "flat as a board" and "mosquito bites" and "itty bitty t***y committee?" Come on, every person on the planet past 11 years old has heard those sayings. The middle school population is obsessed with breasts.

It continues on through high school and college, into adulthood. We're obsessed with breasts. Then, we become mothers and our breasts take on a different meaning. For those who decide to breastfeed, our breasts become a sort of sacred connection with our babies. We feed our babies with them. They represent motherhood.

Then there's society, which has made breasts a focal point in whether or not a female is considered "attractive." Face it, all of us women at one time have thought, "Ugh, I wish my breasts were ... bigger, smaller, rounder, higher (just pick one)." Yes, yes, in theory, we should not worry about our physical appearance and focus on what's inside. But, alas, we are human. We like to be "attractive" to others and, well, ourselves, too. I like to look in the mirror and feel pleased, don't you? My life doesn't depend on it, though.

So, what happens when something happens to our breasts? Something that we have absolutely no control over? Having breast cancer affects women much differently than cancer of any other part of our bodies (except possibly ovaries). I remember when I was growing up in the 1970s. No one talked about breast cancer — until Betty Ford, wife of President Gerald Ford, announced she had breast cancer and had a double mastectomy. I remember hearing a collective gasp from society in thinking her womanly ways were somehow gone because she had no breasts. How sad. Her life is over, some thought. Wait, what? She's a perfectly productive, intelligent woman! But, back then, gender roles were still very traditional. Woman played the gatherer and nurturer who just sat there and looked pretty, while man acted as the hunter and provider. The end.

Yes, we've come a long way. Women are now not as tied to

their gender and bodies for identity, and we have accepted the other gifts we have to become CEOs and world leaders. But some of those more primitive feelings are hard to shake. So maybe we should just acknowledge them. It's okay to feel a fond, womanly attachment to your breasts. Just like men do with their genitalia. We all know most men are overly attached to their own, going so far as to give them nicknames. I can honestly, 100 percent say I've never named my breasts. But yes, they are still my "trusty companions." And that's okay. You're loving a part of you, and what's wrong with that?

It's similar to the feeling a woman gets when she goes through menopause or gets a hysterectomy; or when a man gets a vasectomy or a prostate removal. It is common to feel that your "reason for being," your ability to mate is done. You're washed up, you're old news. We all know it's not true. But, basically, for centuries, a person's worth was based mostly on their ability to produce offspring. It's just a fact. Yes, we have all evolved, but I'll be honest: As I go through perimenopause myself, I feel a bit like I'm losing my worth or my youth. It's silly, I know. Our heads know it's not true. But, let's be honest, we've all felt it. And that's okay.

And this is how I've been told women with breast cancer sometimes feel. I have never had breast cancer, but I have had scares. I've gotten the phone call: "Ms. Madigan, the doctor would like to take some more images." Turns out, so far, I just have lumpy, dense breasts. Great. But I actually remember physically grabbing my breasts and thinking, What would happen if I had to get these babies removed? They make me look better in a dress, they play a role in physical intimacy, they have fed my three children and, most importantly, they are a part of me and I love every part of me.

I'm glad we've evolved and it's not taboo to talk about anymore. The age-old controversy of even uttering the word "breast" has definitely changed. Today, with the increase in breast cancer awareness efforts especially, people even put bumper stickers on their cars and wear bracelets that say, "Save the ta-tas" (which I don't care for, by the way. I find it kind of un-dignifying, but that's just me). I just wanted to take it a step further and explain that, yes, we women hold a special regard for our breasts, and that's okay. It doesn't make us any less or any more of a person. They don't make us smarter or dumber or more or less useful. But we do love our breasts and that's okay, so let's try and show them that love by getting a mammogram, today. I wish you all good health. Remember: Take time to love yourself.

13 USEFUL(LESS) FACTS ABOUT THANKSGIVING

As Elvis Used to Say, "Thank You, Thank You Very Much"

In November, we celebrate Thanksgiving in America. Thanksgiving is supposed to be a time of reflecting and giving thanks... or something. I'm thankful, sure. I have a lot to be thankful for. But I'm not going to be like all those other thoughtful pieces and talk about the importance of giving thanks. So instead of basically writing an article that could just be a motivational poster, I'm going to... give you useful (or useless) facts!

Here in America, as school children we were taught a lovely romantic story about Pilgrims and Native Americans sharing a kumbayah feast together to give thanks. More on that to follow. But did you know that wasn't when Thanksgiving was created? Actually Thanksgiving was fabricated by King Henry VIII (and we know how upstanding he was... Tired of your wife? Kill her and get a new one!) in 1536 during the Reformation in order to compete with the number of holidays the Catholic Church celebrated at the time. So you can thank a Protestant for having the 4th Thursday of November off every year!

However, the storied Thanksgiving celebration that took place in 1621 at the Plymouth Plantation that was attended by roughly 50 Pilgrims and 90 Native Americans (by some accounts) was technically just the first Thanksgiving in America. Not first Thanksgiving ever, though. And that Thanksgiving was not just a one-day affair, it was a three day long festival of sorts. It was three days of hunting, eating, and other entertainment in honor of the colonists' first successful harvest.

And what did they eat at that first Thanksgiving? Nope, not a turkey to be found. The Indians killed five deer as gifts for the colonists, so they ate Bambi at the feast. Along with the venison, they also served Indian corn (seriously), other fowl, barley, and cranberries. However not how we eat cranberry at a modern day turkey dinner where it comes out of a can in a gelatinous blob, or fancily chopped up in a sauce, they ate real raw cranberries, plain. Also, there were no mashed potatoes or pumpkin pie because neither potatoes nor pumpkins had been introduced to New England yet.

Thanksgiving didn't even become a "thing" after that. It wasn't until 1789 when George Washington announced the first ever national Thanksgiving holiday which took place on November 26, 1789. But it didn't become a tradition nationwide until the 19th century. That's when American writer Sara Josepha Hale, most famous for writing the nursery rhyme Mary Had a Little Lamb, was inspired by reading a diary of Pilgrim life to recreate the first Thanksgiving feast. Beginning in 1827, Hale waged a nearly 30-year campaign to make Thanksgiving a national holiday. She also published recipes for mashed potatoes, pumpkin pie, and turkey that would later become staples of the modern-day Thanksgiving dinner.

In 1863, during the Civil War, President Abraham Lincoln declared that the United States would celebrate Thanksgiving every year on the last Thursday in November. But in 1939 President Franklin D. Roosevelt moved the holiday up a week earlier to give Depression-era retailers more time to make money during the pre-Christmas holiday shopping season. Apparently this caused a big kerfuffle, why I'm not really sure. I think some Republicans thought it was an affront to Lincoln's memory. Really? Come on man, and you think people make crazy bi-partisan claims nowadays? Oh boy. Anyway, by 1942 lawmakers passed a resolution making Thanksgiving the fourth Thursday of the month, rather than the last Thursday of the month.

Other Thanksgiving Day traditions: Macy's Thanksgiving Day Parade - In the 1920s, many of Macy's department store employees were first-generation immigrants. Proud of their new American heritage, they wanted to celebrate the American holiday of Thanksgiving with the type of festival their parents had loved in Europe. So in 1924 the first Macy's Thanksgiving Day Parade was held in Manhattan from Central Park to Herald Square and the Macy's flagship store on 34th street. And of course always ending with the appearance of Santa Claus to mark the unofficial start of the Christmas season.

Also Black Friday – the Friday after Thanksgiving, that is another sign of the start of the Christmas season, and the biggest shopping day of the year. The term has two explanations, one is that it started in Philadelphia in the early 60's, the police coined it to describe the heavy and disruptive foot and vehicle traffic downtown on that day. Then retailers caught on because it also meant that sales would go up, thus finally turning a profit and going from "in the red" (operating at a loss) to "in the black" (making a profit). I just think the day is a new way to annoy me with manufactured hype to persuade everyone that they need to be part of the excitement and go out and spend money. Whatever. I don't participate.

And finally other modern traditions – Drunk Uncle Frank who asks you to pull his finger which started around 1974 and the annual Thanksgiving Day Family Brawl episode of Cops which probably started in the late 80's in a trailer park in West Virginia.

And of course, every family has their own traditions and celebrate in their own way and is handed down from generation to generation. I think that's the best part of Thanksgiving. The food is awesome, but the company is better. I think Thanksgiving is my favorite holiday because it has always meant family and friends getting together. This year it is extra special because I now have two kids coming home from college that I haven't seen in months. That is definitely something for which to be thankful.

ABOUT THE AUTHOR

Madge Madigan is a fabulous and somewhat irritable divorced mother of three children – two in pricey colleges and one in high school. Please buy her other book as well, "When Life Gives You Lemons... At Least You Won't Get Scurvy" so that she is able to afford said tuition. When not busy cultivating a master race of well-adjusted successful children, she is Associate Editor and Columnist (obviously) at Rochester Woman Magazine, a nationally known blogger at www.madgemadigan.com and www.divorcedmoms.com and a freelance writer.

25697198R10039

Made in the USA
Middletown, DE
08 November 2015